It Was Written And Engraved:

A series of Essays on Torah, From the Blueprint of Creation to the Transatlantic Slave Trade

Avdiel Ben Levi

Table of Contents

Introduction

Chapter 1:

- How modern Science compliments the Torah
- Elohim: Power/Energy – the positive and negative polarities of Energy (Male and Female)
- The Torah and the letters of the Hebrew Alphabet are the D.N.A of creation

Chapter 2:

- Land of Milk and Honey
- Breath, Spirit, and Soul: 3 levels of Divine attachment
- Africa: a Torah based name

Chapter 3:

- What is the Essence of Wisdom
- El Shaddai: The All Sufficient One
- Mathematical Truths embedded in the Torah

Chapter 4:

- **Righteousness is the Foundation of the Universe**
- **Noah: The first man to be called Righteous**
- **My son, Keep thy Father's commands (Torah)**

Chapter 5:

- Amen vs Amun: Did Egypt (Kemet) influence the way we pray

- Egypt (Mitzraim) means bondage in Hebrew

- The Trans-Atlantic Slave Trade as encoded within the Torah

Acknowledgements

This book is dedicated to my three lovely children: Sari, Sariah, and Amir.

Introduction:

The Torah is a multifaceted text, which not only illuminates the history of many ancient peoples and civilizations, but it also delineates the relationship between G-d and man. As the blueprint of creation, the Torah is viewed as the moral basis and foundation of the Universe itself. Whereas many cultures may have a system of belief which was designed by man to help bring them to a state of righteousness, the Torah is unique insofar as it was designed by G-d Himself, which many nations and cultures testify to, to bring All of man to a state of spiritual and physical perfection, through the empowerment of both learning and applying the Torah in one's life. The sages of the Torah teach that every single world event, both revealed and concealed, are engraved within the very language of Torah - Hebrew. Thus, to unlock the Truths contained within the Torah, one must begin to study the Torah in it's original language, which is Hebrew and begin to unleash various Truths which are embedded within the Torah itself.

This book is composed of a series of essays which I've written on the Torah and the truths it contains. I've inserted essays I've written on several topics within the Torah, which range from: Torah as Science, a Land of Milk and Honey (The Promised Land), the Essence of Wisdom, Morality as the Basis of Life, and lastly The Trans-Atlantic Slave Trade as Encoded within the Torah.

These Truths are designed to empower the reader with a very rich understanding of the Wisdom of the Torah and the prophecies engraved in it, which speak to the conditions of the descendants of the Trans-Atlantic Slave Trade (The West African Diaspora) as well as the intellectual and spiritual legacy of the Torah itself. I implore all who read this book to approach these Truths with an open mind, which is free of racial or cultural bias, for the only way to appreciate the ideas of our fellow man, is to leave and check the subjective ideals we have at the door and enter the room with objective scholarship as the basis of our inquiry.

Chapter 1

Torah as Science:
How modern Science compliments the Torah

As vast as the Universe is and as diffuse as our thoughts are, the story of Creation as told in the Torah is Not Only the most Unique cosmology EVER told, but it is also the ONLY one which agrees with modern Science. In this brief article, I will explain the intrinsic relationship between what Science calls the "Big Bang" and what the Torah calls Berashit בראשית, or In the Beginning.

The Spoken word is the Essential "Creative Force" responsible for all Life forms. As a "Matter" of fact, the Hebrew word for "Speech" is דבר Davar or Daber, which means to Speak and it also means a "Thing" or "Matter". In other words, all words have their own intrinsic shape or form! We learn in Physics that what we call sound is actually 38 thousand beats or vibrations per second, which the brain translates as sound. Light אור however is a vibration which travels at a rate of 400 trillion beats or vibrations per second and this is what the Brain Translates as light. With this knowledge we now know that the Sun "DOES NOT" give light, it ONLY GIVES ENERGY, which is Pure Vibration of Sound, which is then translated in the ether where our Brains translate these vibration frequencies as "Light"! Sound is therefore the "Basis of all Life", for we learn that All Energy originates as a "Vibration" (Sound) and hence the only thing that differentiates all forms of matter is the frequency or rate of vibration within that life form. These Scientific Truths convey & confirm the Torah's Story of Creation, how in the Beginning, G-d the Creator, Spoke (Via Sound,

Articulate & Inarticulate Speech) the Universe into Existence/Being, as it is written: Genesis: 1:3 "And G-d Said, Let there be Light".

The Big Bang theorist Georges Lemaitre was the first to speak of the "Expansion of the Universe", contrary to popular opinion which falsely attributes this discovery to Edwin Hubble, who didn't posit his theories on the expansion of the Universe as observed through his "Hubble" telescope not until two years after Georges Lemaitre said it. Lemaitre also pioneered in applying Einstein's Theory of Relativity to cosmology, or the account of the world's creation.

The Big Bang theory posits that the Universe evolved from an extremely hot and dense estate, which in turn was preceded by a "Big Bang". The Big Bang as Lemaitre theorized, began with a Super subatomic particle, which came into existence from nothing. This Super subatomic particle was an infinitesimal "ball" of protons, protons being the Greek term for "units of light". Time and space as we know it was created instantaneously with the "burst" or emergence of this "light". In this "infinitesimal" ball of light, was all of the matter and energy of the Universe. An astrophysicist comes along and adds irony to the above equation when Peter Higgs, a self-proclaimed atheist, discovers what has now come to be called the "God particle". Photons or light has no mass of its own and the Higgs boson theory postulates that the "God particle", which is also a subatomic structure, comes and gives light it's mass via it's radiating Energy.

Now, just based on the above scientific theoretical observations, we see an intrinsic relationship between the Big Bang theory as told via scientific observation and the cosmology as told through the narrative of Moses in the Torah. For Science describes the primeval state of the Universe as consisting of Nothing. The Torah likewise teaches that the World was created מאין יש Yesh Me'Ayin, or in English: something from nothing. Science also says that the creative spark of the Universe began with an infinitesimal ball of LIGHT (photons), consisting of super subatomic particles, the smallest being protons, which are completely without mass. The Torah likewise teaches that the very first creative manefestation came in the form of Light, as it is written: יהי אור ויהי אור yehi or va'yehi or, Let there be LIGHT - Genesis: 1:3. Science then goes on to state that within this infinitesimal ball of light came an "unknown" source of Energy, ironically termed the "G-d particle", which gave these subatomic structures their mass. Likewise the Torah teaches that Elohim אלהים, which in Hebrew literally means Energy, spoke and the light came into existence from which All matter is based and in Hebrew, the term for spoke, which is davar דבר, also means thing or matter (substance).

Elohim: Energy/Power – The positive and negative polarities of Energy (Male and Female)

The first book of the Torah opens with Genesis Chapter 1 verse 1 which reads: בראשית ברא אלהים את השמים ואת הארץ, which of course in English reads: In the beginning G-d created the Heavens and the Earth. Now, there are those who don't fully understand Hebrew who will attempt to give an authoritative commentary on this verse, without EVER being an authority in the language it was spoken in. For instance the Hebrew word for G-d is Elohim אלהים, which in Hebrew is a "masculine plural" noun. The first part El אל or Eloah אלה, is the singular form of the term for G-d. In Hebrew, the word El אל literally means Power or Energy, as it is written: ידי לאל יש, which in English reads: "It is in the Power of my Hand" (Genesis: 31:29). In this passage, the word for POWER is El אל, which is the singular form of the Hebrew word for G-d אל. Now that we can see that the literal meaning of the Hebrew word for G-d is Power or Energy, we can now understand what the Torah means when it says that Male and Female together comprise the Image of G-d, for we know that there is a Positive polarity of Energy and a Negative polarity of Energy, which in the language of the Torah is termed Male and Female זכר ונקבה.

The last part of the Hebrew word for G-d אלהים, includes the Hebrew letters Yod י and Mem ם, which act as a pluralizing suffix. This is essentially the aspect of the Hebrew word for G-d אלהים, which causes confusion to those who are unfamiliar with Hebrew syntax or grammar. So the argument by those unfamiliar with Hebrew is: Since the Hebrew word for G-d used throughout the first chapter of Genesis is Elohim אלהים, which in essence is a masculine plural word, it then follows that Elohim אלהים more properly indicates more than one G-d ,I.e., "gods", since it stems from a Plural noun. The first problem with this unfounded premise is that it has No base in Hebraic syntax.

When the Torah speaks of G-d אל as Elohim אלהים with a masculine plural, the pluralization indicates immeasurability, Not "multiplicity", as it is written: " to whom will you liken me (G-d) and compare me to that we should be equal" - Isaiah: 40:25.

You see, Biblical Hebrew grammar and syntax, is unlike the language we speak today, therefore in attempting to interpret it we must first divorce our minds from the grammatical rules of every other language we know and speak.

Taking a look at Genesis: 1:1 again, when we encounter the Hebrew word Elohim אלהים, the masculine plurality inherent in its structure, denotes all of the Creative attributes inherent in Creation. From the point of view of Science, these attributes are termed nature, hence the saying "Mother nature". Yet from a purely Hebraic perspective, what is viewed as the "forces of Nature", is termed G-d or Elohim אלהים, hence the Hebrew word for nature which is Ha'Tevah הטבע is numerically equivalent in Hebrew to the word G-d or Elohim אלהים, which is 86 and in Hebraic thought, two words which share numerical equivalence are said to share in conceptual meaning.

Someone may reason that inherent in "nature" there are innumerable forces unseen and seen which underlay and pervade the reality of existence, yet from the point of view of the Torah, All of these forces are exemplified and personified in what is termed G-d or Elohim אלהים.

To further elaborate and conclude my thoughts on this subject we will once again visit Genesis chapter 1. Verse 27 of Genesis chapter 1 reads: ויברא בצלמו האדם את אלהים, which in English means: "and G-d Created man in His image". Hebrew is known as a language of ACTION. In Hebrew, a verb Always precedes a noun, because in Biblical thought what measures a man most is Not who he/She is, But what he/she DOES. Also, when two or more people are DOING (Action) something the verb is pluralizied, hence in Genesis: 1:27, the verb to Create ברא is in the SINGULAR, which let's us know that G-d אלהים

although being immeasurable, is without Plurality, He is SINGULAR. This is what is meant in Deuteronomy: 6:4 where is says: שמע ישראל יהוה אלהינו יהוה אחד, which in English reads: Hear O ' Israel, THE LORD our G-d THE LORD is ONE. And this is also why the last Biblical prophet, Malachi, says: הלוא אב אחד לכלנו הלוא אל אחד בראנו, which in English reads: "Have we All Not ONE FATHER, has Not ONE G-D Created us". This rhetorical question is aimed at us needing to discern that there is Only ONE G-D. This CLEARLY destroys and annuls the false notion or pretense that there are many "gods" and it also conceptually uproots from it's very foundation the notion that the Hebrew word for G-d, Elohim אלהים, denotes the personification of a "multitude" of "gods".

The Torah & the Letters of the Hebrew Aleph Bet are the D.N.A of Creation

The עץ חיים or Tree of life is the basis of the Hebrew Aleph bet. The Torah sages speak of Creation as consisting of 32 paths, hence the first letter of the Torah is the Bet ב of Berashit and the last letter of the Torah is the Lamed ל of Israel, which combined yields 32 and which is the Hebrew word for Heart or Epicenter. The 32 paths are the 22 letters of the Hebrew Aleph Bet and the 10 sayings of Creation. The Creator's Name is mentioned 32 times in the narrative of Creation. The first ten parallel the Ten sayings of Creation, which in turn parallel the Ten commandments.

The other 22 times that the Name G-d or Elohim אלהים appears, parallels the 22 letters of the Hebrew Aleph Bet. The Universe as we know it, is said to be 3 dimensional. When you put 10 lines in 3 dimensional columns, they're automatically linked by 22 lines.

The 22 amino acids are the building blocks of life and therefore the Torah teaches that the 22 letters of the Hebrew Aleph bet are the D.N.A of

Creation, as it is written: "by the word (Words are composed of LETTERS) of G-d the Heavens were made" Psalms: 33:6. Thus the 22 letters of The Hebrew Aleph Bet and the 7 days of Creation fully express the Created Universe, for 22 ÷ 7 = 3.14, which is the mathematical formula for Pi, which measures the Circumference of a Circle, I.e., the Universe!

Chapter 2

Land of Milk and Honey

I would like to share a very random, yet influenced meditation on "Honey" דבש (Dabash) that I had today. As observers of Torah, what do you think about when you "envision" חזה Honey דבש ???

Well, for me, the 1st thing that comes to mind is the Torah's usage of the term "D'bash" דבש (Honey) and how the Torah more often than none, combines it's usage of "Honey" דבש with "Milk" חלב (K'Lev).

Hence, throughout the Torah we find that the "Land of Yisrael" ארץ ישראל is said to "Over-flow" זבת with חלב ודבש "Milk & Honey" (Exodus:3:8, 3:17, 13:5, 33:3, Leviticus:20:24, Numbers:13:27, 14:8, Deuteronomy: 6:3, 11:9, 26:9, 27:3, Joshua:5:6, Jeremiah:32:22).

Honey and Milk, are regarded in the Medical community as a "Complete Food" אכל תם, Honey דבש containing Every essential mineral and vitamin necessary to sustain life and promote immune health; with Milk חלב containing nutritious properties which strengthens teeth, bones, and muscles. So, in a sense, Honey דבש heals and strengthens the "interior" while Milk חלב heals and strengthens the "exterior".

The words of Torah דברי התורה are also compared to Milk חלב and Honey דבש, as it is written: "Honey drips from your lips... Honey and Milk lies under your Tongue" (Song of Songs: 4:11). In this passage, King Solomon equates the "Spiritually healing" properties of the Torah תורה and it's Interpretation קבלה to the

"Physically healing" properties of Milk and Honey. Also, both words in a Hebrew for Milk and Honey חלב ודבש, stem from Hebraic roots which mean to "Fatten or Thicken", and alludes to the In-depth interpretation of Torah, which is shrouded or layered with meaning.

Psalm: 19 verses 8-11 defines "6 ways" that the Torah, which was given to Israel on the 6th of Sivan, for Man who was created on the 6th day of creation, and interpreted via the Mishna, which has 6 Sedarim (Chapters), can Heal, Strengthen, Nourish, Sustain, Edify, and Spiritually empower Man to do G-d's will, which is the Torah. In fact, to say "His (G-d's) Will" in Hebrew is "Rat'zon" רצון and "His (G-d's) Name" in Hebrew is "Shay'mo" שמו which are both numerically equivalent to the number 346, which is the numerical equivalence of חלב דבש Milk and Honey in Hebrew… For 2 things were revealed in the era of the Exodus: which was the giving of the Law (His Will) רצון and the revelation of the Most Divine Name mentioned in the Torah יהוה "YHVH" (His Name) שמו and it was from there that we journeyed to the Land of Yisrael ארץ ישראל a land flowing with "Milk and Honey".

Breath, Spirit, and Soul: 3 levels of Divine attachment

In order to understand the difference between Nishma נשמה and Ruach רוח, one must first come to understand that the Torah mentions three levels of Soul, each higher than the other. The three levels of Soul which the Torah mentions are: Nishma נשמה, Ruach רוח, and Nefesh נפש. Nishma נשמה in Hebrew literally means breath. Ruach רוח in Hebrew literally means Wind. And lastly, Nefesh נפש in Hebrew literally means to rest or settle, as in the place where Wind is gathered and settles.

The best way to discern the unique differences between these three levels of Soul, is to introduce the Glass blower analogy. When Glass is made, it begins with the Breath (Nishma) of the Blower, as this breath travels, it's Wind (Ruach) causes the very shape of the vessel to contract and expand, where it finally fills the entire breadth of the vessel and Settles or Rests (Nefesh) there.

In this analogy, we can discern three Torah based truths about our Soul and its various levels. An East wind (Ruach) can be felt thousands of miles from its source, while in order to feel someone's breath (Nishma), you have to be in front of or connected to the source. This is essentially the difference between Nishma נשמה and Ruach רוח. Nishma is the very breath of G-d, as such it is still connected to Him, which is its source of Life. Ruach however, implies a lower level of Spiritual connectivity, as it represents a more distanced spiritual relationship with G-d. Nefesh נפש, which is the lowest level of our Souls, is directly connected to our fleshly being and hence susceptible to our carnal lusts and desires. Whenever the Torah speaks of the Soul that Sins (Ezekiel:18), it is speaking of our Nefesh or animalistic nature. For when a person reaches the level of Ruach Hakodesh, which is Prophecy, his Soul has freed itself from the bounds of Sin, which entails that if they were to sin from that point on (Ruach), it was Not intentional. Yet, when a person reaches the awareness of their highest level of Soul, known as Nishma נשמה, they have conquered Sin itself, which leads to my conclusion.

When Moses ascended Mount Nebo הור נבו, our sages teach that he conquered Sin itself, as he achieved an awareness of the Highest level of his Soul, known as Nishma נשמה. In fact, the very name of the Mount Moses Ascended, encapsulates the fact that Moses attained the highest spiritual experience, just before dying. For the name Nebo נבו, doesn't just mean prophet in Hebrew, when viewed as a compound word, Nebo נבו literally means, the Nun (Nishma) is within him. In fact, as proof of this, if we add the letter Nun נ to Moses's name משה, it can then be rearranged to spell Nishma נשמה.

Africa: a Torah based Name

When pursuing Truth, it's best to totally separate one's self from any form or semblance of bias views or attitudes, as this will corrupt and distort the purity within the Truths you desire to apprehend. That being said, I'd like to offer some critical research on the origin of the term "Africa or African".

According to urban rhetoric, the name Africa is derived from the Roman General Publius Cornelius Scipio, otherwise known as Scipio

Africanus. However, genuinely critical analysis and research reveals that prior to the "Punic Wars", fought by Rome against the Great Master Military General, Hannibal of Carthage, Scipio's full birth name was Publius Cornelius Scipio! Upon the defeat of Hanibal by the Young Roman General Publius Cornelius Scipio, he was nicknamed by Rome "Scipio Africanus", after the name of the land/region that the people of Hannibal populated.

Hannibal was not a native of Carthage, which is today's modern Libya. Instead, Hannibal migrated to Carthage (Libya) from Palestine as he was a descendant of the ancient Phonecians, who were displaced by the Children of Israel after years of political and social conflict and were later forced into exile to the "vassal state" of Carthage (Libya) in North Africa. According to the Roman historian Besorus, the people who inhabited North Africa called themselves "Afri" עפרי and hence upon the defeat of Hannibal, Scipio became known in Rome as the "Roman Hannibal", where he developed the nickname Scipio Africanus; a name (Africa/Afri/עפרי) which reflects the region of land Hannibal reigned from.

According to Josephus Flavius, who lived between 37 C.E - 100 C.E, the name of Africa is derived from "Opher" עפר, the grandson of Abraham avinu (our forefather) Genesis: 25:4.

In Josephus' book of Antiquities, Josephus revisits the biblical genealogies of Shem, Ham, and Yapheth.

He asserts that the name "Africa " עפריך is derived from "Opher" עפר the grandson of Abraham, who conquered the Egyptian descended Libyans (Genesis:10:13), and renamed the land after himself - "Opher" עפר, hence its name now and during the time of Hannibal - Africa פרידע which means in Hebrew, the land of Opher (Antiquities:15:239-240).

In summary, what is most important here is the notion that Africa's name is Not of Roman Origin, but of Hebraic/Biblical origin.

Scipio "Africanus", was Only named such (Africanus), to comemorate his defeat of Hannibal the African, who inhabited the land of Africa/"Afri" עפרי.

Prior to his defeat of Hannibal, his name was exclusively as Publius Cornelius Scipio!

The truths conveyed above are so important to a student of the Torah, who should always have in his or her possession, the clearest possible view of Truth as the Torah is thee standard by which Truth is measured.

Chapter 3

What is the Essence of Wisdom

While many, may hold the notion that the Apprehension of Wisdom constitutes a state of mind where because of the maturation of the Thought/Wisdom they possess, that they are no longer subject to further inquiry into the Truths they consider to be "Intellectually Concrete", I beg to differ. The analogy the Torah draws depicts for Wisdom is Always Water! Wisdom is compared to Water in the Torah because just as Water is without "Solidity", so is Wisdom without Limitation and just as Water is Life-giving, so is the Torah likened to a "Fountain of Living Waters", from which the depths of her well brings forth Life-Everlasting!

The Hebrew word for Wisdom is "Chochmah" חכמה, "Chochmah" (Wisdom) in Hebrew is actually a compound Word. It is composed of two Hebrew words: חכ and מה (Choch and Mah). חכ "Choch" in Hebrew means "Strength or Power" and Mah מה is the Hebrew word for "What", which is a "Question".... Therefore

חכמה "Chochmah", the Hebrew word for Wisdom, actually means when broken down "Hebraically", the "Power כח "Choch" to Question מה "Mah". You see, Wisdom essentially means to "Question All Things", therefore is says in the Mishna: Pirkei Avot Chapter 4 verse 1: איזהו חכם הלומד מכל אדם - "Who is Wise" ? Answer: He who Learns from Everyone! This is why it says in the Psalms: "From All my Teachers I grew Wise" Psalms: 119:99. But let's get even deeper than this....

Have you ever wondered why in English the Words " What " and " Water " are linguistically similar ? You Cannot say "Water", without saying "What"! So then, for those who study etymology and linguistics, what is the "Conceptual Relationship" between the Words "What and Water" ?

In Hebrew, the word for "What" is Mah מה and the word for "Water" is Mayim מים. Just as in English, the Two words for "What & Water" in Hebrew stem from the same "Etymological Roots"! So again what is the significance? When we ask a question, what essentially are we saying or implying? We asking questions to bring clarity to things that our minds cannot grasp (Touch)! Water is like a question. Take your hands and try to pick up water, can you hold it? No! Water cannot be grasped, unless it is sunk into a depth (understanding).

This is why in the proverbs King Solomon says: "Wisdom is like a Well and Only a Man of Understanding can draw it out". So, just as Water cannot be grasped, so it is that we only ask questions about an Idea or Concept that our minds cannot touch (Grasp). This is the etymological significance of the relationship of the

"Etymological Roots" for the Hebrew & English words for Water מים and What מה.

El Shaddai: The All Sufficient One

The Biblical title G-d Almighty/El Shaddai שדי אל, signifies an "Attribute" of the creator, as the sustainer and nourisher of All life. As the milk of a mother sustains the life of her young, so is the Creator said to be a source of sustenance both physically and spiritually to man.

Those ignorant of the Creator's many attributes and what they genuinely delineate, foolishly reason that since the designation El Shaddai has feminine connotation, then El

Shaddai must be independent of the G-d of the Bible and hence must be His female counterpart. While none of these Assumptions are founded upon scholarship in the Hebrew language or doctrine of the Torah.

The Torah emphatically states that implicit in the term or designation Elohim, is a Male and Female energy, hence the Hebrew word Elohim אלוהים, literally means Energy or Power in Hebrew and in particular, positive and negative energy, which in the language of biological gender differences are termed, Male or Female, hence the Torah says: and G-d formed man in His image בצלמו,

Male and Female He created them. Hence, the Divine attribute Elohim אלוהים, which in Hebrew means Power or Energy is implicit of both the positive (male) and negative (female) polarities of Energy. Yet, the Torah still says: שמע ישראל יהוה אלהינו יהוה אחד, Here O' Israel, YHVH our Power, YHVH is one.

Mathematical Truths Embedded in The Torah

The sages of the Torah taught that G-d's Name El Shaddai שדי אל comes from the fact that as the Universe began to unfold, uniformly in All directions creating an infinite circle, according to His will, as soon as it reached the point of His will's satisfaction, He said Enough/Dai די in HEBREW.

What is exceptionally significant about the creation of this infinite circle, known in Hebrew as Olam עולם, meaning the Universe, is that according to Science, the mathematical term "Pi", which measures the circumference of a circle, has a material formula of 3.14.

Our Ancient sages however, long before the mathematical discovery of "Pi", stated that the Divine Name El Shaddai שדי אל, is what brought the Universe (Infinite Circle) to a halt! The numerical equivalence or Sacred Geometry of Shaddai שדי in Hebrew is EXACTLY 314, which is the mathematical formula for "Pi", which "measures" the Circumference of All circles. Hence, look Not to Egypt's Pyramid for Sacred Geometry, for encoded within the very Language of the Torah, is the Sacred Geometry of Consciousness (Truth). Thus El Shaddai שדי אל signifies He who sets a limit on His creations and endows All of creation according to It's sufficiency, as well as he who set a limit to the unfolding of the Universe (Infinite Circle) with His Divine Attribute of El Shaddai שדי אל, of which is encoded one of the Greatest mathematical principles known to Man – Pi, which is identical to the Encoded Geometry of the Divine Name used at the advent of creation, El Shaddai שדי אל.

Chapter 4

Morality is the basis of Life,

"Righteousness is the foundation of the Universe"

(Proverbs:10:25)

It's Never "too late" to "re-discover" the righteousness צדק "inherent" within you, for according to Genesis בראשית Chapter:1:26, we were created ברא in the Image of G-d אלוהים בצלם; which entails that "Righteousness" צדק is built into our "Spiritual D.N.A". However, in contra-distinction to these Truths, there is a logic of "self-defeat" which is very prevalent among us and it dictates that when we "Sin" חטא, we fall נפל short of G-d's Glory כבוד אלוהים and thus can Never "Truly" attain the "Perfection" תמימה we were designed to achieve. This "pseudo-logic" couldn't be Any further removed from Truth.

Before anything was created ברא, "Darkness" חושך was at the Genesis of the very point from which creation sprang forth. In comes G-d אלוהים who reveals the Torah תורה (Light) as the "Nexus" of the Spiritual

"Inner-space" and the Physical Outer-space".

This light האור ואת *התורה* את (Genesis:1:4) first manifests herself from the inner-depths of "Darkness" חושך itself, to bring forth "Life" *תורה* as the "foundation" upon which All of creation *בריה* "stands"! So hence, from the outset, Nothing can "Truly" be said to be "Good"/"Perfect", until it undergoes (Is tested) a "spiritual transformation" from the depths of "Darkness/Sin" וחטא חושך. Just as "Darkness" preceeds "Light", so does a state of "Sin" preceed that of "Righteousness", as it is written: "for there is No "Righteous" man

צדיק who does "Good" טוב and does Not "Sin" "חטא (Ecclesiastes:7:20).

The Torah תורה is in a sense, designed to "restore" משיבת spiritual balance. One of the main spiritual faculties of "Torah-observance", is "restoration" משיבת of spirit, as it is written: משיבת תמימה יהוה תורה נפש - The "Teaching/Law" of LORD is perfect תמימה "restoring" משיבת the Soul נפש (Psalms:19:8).

No matter how low we or the world may perceive us, as a result of the sins we've committed, there is

Always room to get up and return שובה to the higher spiritual estate inherent in our very design. Unlike the religious dogma which plagues many people around the world, arrogating to the uninformed mind that once you've sinned the Salvation inherent in Torah observance is lost to you; we, those of us who "genuinely" Know Torah, Truly understand the fallacy and short comings of such an uninformed statement on Torah.

The Torah תורה "enables" us to transform "Darkness" (Sin) חטא into "Light" (Righteousness) צדק, Torah observance is like a rich assortment of Vitamins and Minerals which empowers the mind and body to perceive and achieve greatness!

Do not let your short-comings define you, instead allow your steadfast courage and Trust in G-d's word (Torah) to redefine you continually until you are restored to the original mold and shape you were designed under צדק (righteousness).

It's known that Man will sin (Ecclesiastes: 7:20), that goes without question! No great leader or teacher is immune to the temptations of sin, however, what defines you most, is your ability to "withstand" sin as much as is in your power, for it is Not the sin which will break you, but your "refusal" to reconnect the pieces (get up and return to G-d).

Noah –
The first man to be Called righteous

The Torah says with regard to Noah, just before the "Epic Flood of the World" took place, that "Noah Found "GRACE" חֵן in the Eyes of God (YHVH)" Genesis: 6:8. This is the very first time that the Torah speaks of Grace!

The Torah now goes on to tell us how Noah found "Grace" חֵן in God's (YHVH's) eyes, meaning that the Torah gives us a "Clear" & "Concise" definition of what Noah did in order to merit or "Earn" God's (YHVH's) Grace! As it is written: "Noah was a Righteous צדיק Man, PERFECT תמים in his generations and he (Noah) "Walked with God (YHVH)" Genesis:6:9.

Immediately we see "Two" things which call for a more in-depth explanation; the first thing is the term "Righteous" צדיק. This is Also the Very FIRST Time that the Torah uses the term "Righteous" צדיק. So far what is highly significant to note is that the Very 1st time the Torah "Introduces" the word "Grace" חן it also introduces the word "Righteous" צדיק. This comes to Teach us that there is a Spiritual relationship between the concept of "Grace חן & Righteousness" צדק.

The Hebrew word for Righteousness is "Tzedek" צדיק (Spelled - Tzade + Dalet + Yod + Qoph). From studying the base of this word we find that it differs greatly from how it is used today.

For instance, the dictionary says "Righteousness" צדק is the act of being Just, Upright, or administering Justice. However, since we know that

Hebrew ALWAYS reveals the greatest depth of Language, let's see what righteousness "Literally" means in Hebrew.

As we saw above, righteousness in Hebrew is the word צדיק Tzadek or Tzedek, it is spelled (Tzade + Dalet + Yod + Qoph). The etymological dictionary of Biblical Hebrew says that the base or foundational "Root letters" of Tzedek is Tzadah צדה (Tzadeh + Dalet + Hey). Tzadah צדה in Hebrew means to hunt or "Pursue"; the second half of the word Tzadek צדק is the "Single letter" Qoph ק in Hebrew. Qoph is the

Initial letter of the word Quadosh קדוש in Hebrew, which means "Holiness". So then, putting two words together, we see that Tzadek צדק means "To Pursue Holiness". This then is the meaning of the Torah telling us: "Righteousness, Righteousness, shall you "PURSUE" Deuteronomy:16:20.

So "Righteousness" literally means in Hebrew, "To Pursue Holiness". This being Clarified, we also know that "Righteousness" represents living by God's Law (Torah), as it is written: "And it (the Torah) will be counted as "Righteousness" for us, if we are careful to observe All of the

Commandments (Torah)"
Deuteronomy:6:25

So as we learned above, Noah Only found "Grace", which is Salvation (as he (Noah) was "Saved from the Flood Waters), by virtue of the Fact that he kept the Torah! For the verse states that Noah "Walked" with God (YHVH) and the Torah is known as "Halacha" הלכה in Hebrew, which literally means "The Path one Walks"!

Lastly, here is an even bigger question.... How did Noah keep God's Law (Torah) when it wasn't revealed until Moses 16 generations after

Noah? Here is a hint, the Torah says with regard also to Abraham: "Abraham obeyed MY voice, and observed MY commandments, my decrees, and My Torah" Genesis: 26:5. AGAIN, if the Torah wasn't given until 6 generations after Abraham, how can the Torah say Abraham kept the Entire revealed Torah?

In the book of Proverbs, King Solomon speaks about Wisdom. In the 8th Chapter King Solomon speaks on the Role of Wisdom in Creation. The 3rd chapter of Proverbs says: "With Wisdom God founded the Earth" Proverbs: 3:19. Now, the 8th chapter of Proverbs speaks about this in detail: "When He (God) created the Foundations of the Earth, I (Wisdom) was his "Nursling" (Amon in Hebrew) אמון. Don't read "Amon" אמון (Nursling), but instead read "Uman" אומן (Architect)! For the scrolls of the Torah are written without vowel points, so this word more properly means "Architect" (Uman) and fits perfectly with the intent of the Author (King Solomon). For King Solomon is teaching us that Wisdom was the "Creative Tool" in God's Hand! But what is Wisdom?

Wisdom is the Torah, as it is written: "This (The Torah) is your Wisdom in the sight of the people" Deuteronomy: 4:6. Also, because I'm a person who loves depth, every letter in the Hebrew Alphabet has a numerical equivalent; Aleph א equals 1 & Bet ב equals 2 etc.

When the Hebrew word for Wisdom (Chochmah) חכמה is spelled out with each letter in the Word "individually", the Equivalent is 613 (Torah) -------> Khet ח 8 + Yod 10 י + Tav 400 ת + Caph 20 כ + Peh 80 פ + Mem 40 מ + Yod 10 י + Mem 40 מ + Hey 5 ה equals 613 (Number of Commandments in the Torah).

"My Son, Keep thy Father's commands (Torah)"

Proverbs:6:20

There are two letters in Hebrew which form the word for Father, which is Abba אב. The first letter is Aleph א which means to Teach. The second letter is Bet ב, which means House in Hebrew; so the complete thought formed in the Hebrew word for Father אב, is that a Father is the Teacher of his house. As such what defines Fatherhood is Not just the "Seed" which you implant within a Woman, but it is the "Seed of Truth" Jeremiah:2:21 אמת זרע, which you implant within your home, in the minds of your children. The greatest gift that you can give a child is Not that which is tangible, it's that which is intangible to the hand, yet very palpable to the mind!

G-d likewise is our Father, as He created us All. Yet, just as above, what defines G-d as our Father, is Not essentially the "Breath of Life" which He gave us All, but instead it is the Teaching of Truth תורת אמת (TORAH) Malachi:2:6, which He implanted within our Minds, which defines G-d as our Father. It is Good to "believe" in G-d, yet if you Don't acknowledge His Teachings (TORAH), then in essence you do Not acknowledge Him as your Father, which is a title indicative of imparting Truth/Wisdom to one's children!

We were created in His (G-d's) image, to emulate His Truths, hence the Only way to acknowledge Him is to emulate what He conveyed and left on record for us.

Chapter 5

Amen vs Amun

Did Egypt (Kemet) influence the way we Pray?

Whenever we employ subjective thought in our pursuit of Truth, we will always be subject to the suppression of Truth for the sake of our biased agenda(s).

Therefore, the very best way to approach ascertaining Truth, is to distance ourselves from any subjective point of view, with regard to the information we endeavor to research and unearth.

For quite some time now in our recent history, there's been much unfounded information circulating and maliciously propagated against the veracity of the Truths and Teachings which originate in the Torah, some of which range from claims of: plagiarism, unreliability of Biblical history, insufficient archaeological records, etc.

I'm not here to say that people aren't entitled to having an adverse view or opinion, No, conversely What I'm here to say is: We are All allowed to have whatever points of view which our minds carve for us based on the information we gravitate towards, yet the Only ones which will be respected as Authoritative and Intellectually "significant", are those points of view which are merited in "Genuine" research and "Scholarly" labor. With that being said, I will now talk about the Biblical origin and meaning of the term Amen אמן, which is primarily used in prayer.

Google, with all of its increasing benefits, still has a semblance of distortion and confusion, because virtually any article published on the internet, can and will appear on Google search, thus the birth of the "Google scholar". Google, among other similar entities, has changed the intellectual landscape of genuine scholarship.

In the so called "conscious" community, you have pseudo scholars, from the prestigious academies of Google and Wikipedia, who will dare to look into the Torah and give a pseudo definition of terms which should only be expressed or quantified through scholarship in the doctrine of the Torah as well as the language (Hebrew) of the Torah.

Through artifice cunning, these Google and Wikipedia pseudo scholars, have introduced the faulty premise that the Hebrew word Amen אָמֵן, comes out of Kemet, the Home of Amen Ra. This unfounded attempt of linguistic scholarship, doesn't take into account that the Name or term Amen as used in Ancient Kemet (Egypt) is of a much later development. The original name and term is actually "Amun", according to many Egyptologist, But in particularly Dr. Ben Yochanan, a renowned Afrocentric scholar of Kemet history, civilization, and doctrine. Amun in Kemetic language means hidden and refers to unseen forces or powers.

Therefore, in order for this premise to be True, the Hebrew word Amen אמן, must Not only sound the same (linguistics), But it also must have a similar meaning. So let's open the Torah and explain All of the usages/meanings of Amen אמן.

The very first time that the Hebrew word Amen אמן appears in the Torah is when G-d יהוה promises Abraham that He will have his own seed (Children), and the Torah says: "and Abraham believed והאמן in G-d יהוה and it was ascribed to Abraham as righteousness" - Genesis: 15:6. The Hebrew word for belief or trust is

אמן Amen. The Hebrew root word Amen אמן appears a total of 65 times in the Torah. Whenever the root Amen אמן appears in the Torah, it has one of three etymological meanings, which are: belief, trust, and contract/covenant. Thus, in the book of Nehemiah: 10:1, Amen אמן is used as the word for covenant, in this instance denoting a written contract.

Throughout the book of Psalms, we also find Amen אמן used to denote the confirmation of an act or pronouncement, this time in the form of an "Oral contract": Psalms:

41:14, 72:19, 89:53, 106:48, etc. In the book of Numbers: 12:7, Amen אמן is used to denote Trust, in describing The Superior prophetic status of Moses, above all the Prophets of the Torah. In all of the above Torah based usages, NOWHERE can we find "Amun", or the implication of Amen meaning hidden force or power.

This is a crucial point in objective research, you can begin with any premise you want, but when the evidence doesn't match your premise, the scholarly effort has reached its termination and conclusion.

Egypt means Bondage in Hebrew, Let's prove it!

When one attains scholarship in a particular area of Truth, it's easy to discern a novice from an initiate.

Therefore, it is the responsibility of those whom are astute in a particular branch of Truth, to reject the pseudo-scholarship of those whom are attempting to exercise some semblance of authority in it, without having the appropriate scholarship in it. As a fluent Biblical Hebrew סופר scholar, I don't allow anyone in my presence to speak authoritatively on the Hebrew language, without exemplifying some basic baseline scholarship in it. We cannot allow anyone to tell us what our language conveys. As teachers of Hebraic vernacular, we are the authority and therefore we will tell those who exist outside of the Hebraic barometers what our language conveys, not vice versa. As we draw near to putting Kemet on trial, I will slowly but surely dispel many of the myths that they arrogate to themselves and others. That being noted, let's talk about the Hebrew word for Egypt and define it Hebraically. The Hebrew word for Egypt is Mitzraim מצרים, which is a masculine plural noun in

Hebrew. It stems from a Hebraic root which means to bind (shackle or imprison), to be bound or a boundary, and lastly it means bondage, servitude, or slavery. The above descriptions align perfectly with the Torah's appellations and synonyms for Ancient Egypt or Kemet. Within the Torah, Egypt known in Hebrew as Mitzraim מצרים, is synonymous with BONDAGE and servitude (Slavery).

There are at least 13 references in the Torah to Egypt מצרים as being the House of Bondage:

Exodus:13:3,

Exodus:13:14,

Exodus:20:2,

Deuteronomy:5:6,

Deuteronomy:6:12,

Deuteronomy:7:8,

Deuteronomy:8:14,
Deuteronomy:13:6,
Deuteronomy:13:11,

Joshua:24:17,

Judges:6:8,

Jeremiah:34:13,

Micah:6:4

So whenever Egypt or in Hebrew Mitzraim is mentioned in the Torah, it is synonymous with physical and mental Bondage (Slavery).

The common mind will view the above as slander, as opposed to viewing it from the spectacles of those (Hebrews) who endured it (Slavery in Egypt).

Do remember, outside of Kemet (Egypt), the Torah is one of thee 'ONLY' primary sources which preserves the ancestral Name of Egypt. The name Egypt is of Greek origin, coming from the Greek word Aegyptos, which is a Greek transliteration of the Kemetic phrase: Het-Ka-Ptah. Het means place and Ka means: "the physical projection of the soul", not the body, which is the character or aura that attaches itself to the body. Yet, the Ancient peoples of "Egypt", referred to themselves as "Khem", the "T" sound of Keme(t), being a much later derivation, hence they originally spoke of themselves as the people of Khem, which in the Medu Neter means the Black land, alluding to the fertile soil around the Nile river, which as it flooded annually, left Rich alluvial deposits of thick BLACK soil.

Well, guess what… The Torah refers to Egypt as the land of Kham חם as well Psalms:105:23, except when the Torah does so, it takes it a step further into the annals of History, for the biblical Kham חם is the father or progenitor of Mitzraim מצרים (Egypt/Kham - Genesis:10:6). So not only does the Torah preserve the ancestral Name of Ancient Khemet (Egypt), But it also names its founding father, the Biblical Kham חם and gives us the True name of Egypt which is Mitzraim מצרים. This is why, all of the Asiatic kingdoms refer to Egypt/Khemet as Misar (Arabic), Mitzraim (Hebrew), & Mistre (Cuneiform/Babylonian). This points to the fact that the Semitic Kingdoms have a much older and accurate tradition of Khemet's True lineage, ancestry, and origin.

One of the meanings of Mitzraim or Egypt in Hebrew is a boundary or strait. Yet, when closely assessing or examining the root word in Hebrew for Mitzraim מצרים, we see a much deeper meaning. The sages of the Torah teach that most of the names listed in the Table of Nations in Genesis chapter 10, contain a prophecy which is implicit in there very Name. Thus Egypt or Khemet חמת, is known in the Torah as Mitzraim because Ancient Khemet would grow to be a place which spiritually and physically enslaved many people's and nations and the duality or plurality in its Hebraic root, conveys the idea that there would rise a Nation (America) who would emulate the Ancient practices of Khemet and use it to again enslave many nations. For the word Mitzraim מצרים in Hebrew is based on a trilateral root, which is Mtzr מצר, which literally in Hebrew means to bind with a rope (imprison) as well as literally denoting a Slave or Slavery.

The Trans Atlantic Slave Trade, as encoded within the Torah

Those who base their faith on the Torah or what is known as the Bible, emphatically attest to the idea that the Creator reveals His will to His servants the Prophets, as it is written: The LORD will Not do ANYTHING, unless He reveals His secret to His servants the Prophets - Amos:3:7. Everything in the Universe is in the hand of G-d. While man may attribute a turn in history to a Righteous or Wicked King or Ruler, the Torah says: "Like streams of Water is the heart of a king in the hand of G-d, whatever He (G-d) wills or desires, so He directs it" - Proverbs: 21:1. Thus, the chain or course of events as played out in History, is meticulously moved by the Will of G-d. With that being said, for the Trans-Atlantic Slave Trade to have occurred, clearly it was the will of G-d.

The Torah is thee ONLY literary work, which answers the questions of why Slavery occurred, why G-d allowed it and who or what is the True National identity of the Slaves of the Trans Atlantic Slave Trade. In the book of Deuteronomy chapter 28, Moses is told by G-d to give us an exhortation about the spiritual necessity of aligning ourselves with His (G-d's) will. Verses 1-14, teaches and empowers us with an understanding of how the Torah gives us spiritual identity. We are taught in these verse that we will be blessed in many ways if we keep the commands of G-d. HOWEVER, verses 15 - 68, exhorts us against not aligning ourselves to the will of the G-d. We are taught that the opposite of being blessed by virtue of keeping G-d's law, is being cursed for not keeping it. To the point of the destruction of Not just our spiritual identity, But our physical identity as well. For the sake of not letting too much information out of my bag and for the sake of saving them for a greater platform of which to proclaim them, my proofs of a prophecy which speaks to us as a people, as descendants of the Trans Atlantic Slave Trade, will focus on ONLY 2 verses from Deuteronomy: Chapter 28.

In order to bring you up to speed with my mode of interpretation, I will present some examples of the esoteric depth of the Hebrew language. Every Hebrew letter has a numerical equivalent, similar to Roman numerals. For instance, Aleph א equals 1, Bet ב equals 2, and Gimmel ג equals 3. So the word for

Pregnancy in Hebrew is Ha'riyon הריון, which is numerically equivalent to 271 in Hebrew. What's so special about that? Well, from fertilization to delivery is 270 or 271 days according to Science; for the average month consists of 30 days and some 31, while the term of Pregnancy on Average is 9 months, hence 9 × 30 is 270 and since on average some months have 31 days, Science says the average term is 271 days, which ironically is the numerical equivalence of the Hebrew word for Pregnany, Ha'riyon הריון. Similarly, the Hebrew word for father is Av אב (1+2), which is numerically equivalent to 3. The Hebrew word for mother is Ema אם (1+40), which is numerically equivalent to 41. What's so significant about this? Well, the union of parents brings children, so the Hebrew word for Child is Yeled ילד (10+30+4), which is numerically equivalent to 44, which is the combined values in Hebrew for Father אב 3 and Mother אם 41 = 44. Hebrew is a language with great conceptual depth, encoded in the Hebrew language are the discoveries of modern Science, Ancient History, as well as Prophecy. With this in mind, Lets look at Deuteronomy: 28:68 first...

The very last curse described in Deuteronomy: 28:68, which was suppose to represent the total destruction of our physical and spiritual identity as a people, says: "and the LORD יהוה shall bring you into Egypt again, this time by way of Ship and there you shall offer yourselves for Sale to your enemies.... No, other people, other than those who were taken through the middle passage via The Trans Atlantic Slave Trade, can attest to this description! The Torah teaches in Deuteronomy 28, that the reason we are cursed as a people and were forced into slavery is because we did Not Keep G-d's laws, which are the

613 commandments which G-d gave Moses. The very first Slave ship to Sail to America with Slaves, was captained by Sir John Hawkins and the Name of his ship was ספינה ישוע טובה The Good Ship Jesus. In Hebrew, the Good Ship Jesus is ironically numerically equivalent to 613 טובה ספינה ישוע, the very number of commandments G-d gave Moses which He said if we didn't Keep would lead to us being placed on Ships via Slavery...... Coincidence ?

Lastly, in Deuteronomy: 28:49, G-d describes the Nations which would enslave us, by saying: "The LORD

יהוה will carry a Nation against you from afar, from the End of the Earth, as an EAGLE (America's National Symbol) flies, a Nation whose language you will Not understand".... And guess what.... The numerical equivalence in Hebrew of a Nation "whose language you will Not understand", לשנו תשמע לא, is 1227, which is also the numerical equivalence in Hebrew of: עבדים סחר אטלנטית הטרנס The Trans Atlantic Slave Trade, in Hebrew – TALK TO ME !!!

Conclusion

The world is full of Keys and Locks, one for Revelation and one for Concealment, yet All for the Glory of G-d! The Torah is a vast and deep Sea, therefore be prepared to dive in if you seek to probe its depth. Yet be mindful of the Universal yet paradoxical Truth, the deeper you dive into the Sea of Wisdom, the greater your chances of drowning in it. Moderation is key, no matter what lock is before you. Yet be not afraid to reach the depths of Wisdom, simply because of your fears, instead practice like a Master craftsman before delving through each depth. And above All, be Not afraid to seek what others have yet to find. Be Not afraid to question around those who regard you as too deep, perhaps they are themselves too shallow to comprehend the essence of life's depths!

I would like to Thank all of the pioneers from my community, who paved the way for me to have a voice today, I Thank: Rabbi Arnold Josiah Ford, Rabbi Arthur Wentworth Mathews, Nabi Raphael, Cohen Levi of Hashabba and B'nai Adath, Cohen Michael Ben Levi, my teachers: Nasi

Tzippor Ben Zevulun, who helped me to establish my spiritual base by empowering me with my cultural identity and helping me to instill at a very early age, the discipline which was necessary for me to thrive from youth to adulthood. Chief of Chiefs: Chief Naphtali Ben Naphtali, who to date is the most eloquent soul I have EVER met. A man of great intellectual stature, who takes the words of Torah and meticulously implants them in the minds of those who are willing to hear them. You by far have been a Major influence in my life and I am honored that you were an instrument in the hands of the Almighty G-d, who used you to help me form a way with words and take speech and eloquently carve out Truth.

Lastly, to Crown Prince Tzurishaddai Ben Yehudah, for teaching me several Torah based truths and unearthing the depth of Torah learning, who would always say to me: "a Hint to the Wise is Sufficient". I Thank congregation Beth Ab Shalom of Brooklyn, New York, the very first congregation I EVER attended. I also would like to thank the congregation Sh'ma Yisrael, also of Brooklyn, New York, for nurturing me at such a young age (15/16 yrs.' old) and empowering me with the Truth of my spiritual and physical identity.

CPSIA information can be obtained
at www.ICGtesting.com
Printed in the USA
BVHW041103011218
534519BV00020B/792/P